I AM SHERIAUNA

BOOK 1: We Are Beautiful

Written by: Sherylee Honeyghan

Illustrated by: Ana Patankar

Publication date March 2017
Printed by CreateSpace

ISBN 9781540861962

"For you formed my inward parts; You covered me in my mother's womb. I will praise you, for I am fearfully and wonderfully made; Marvelous are Your works, and that my soul knows very well."

- Psalms 139:13-14 NKJV

To my beautiful Princess Sheriauna. God was preparing me for you and He knew what He was doing when He created you. You are special because God made you that way! Continue to shine and sparkle wherever you go and leave your mark on the minds and hearts of whoever you meet my sweet girl.

Love always and forever, Mommy.

Note to Parents/Guardians/Caregivers:

I hope that you and your child (ren) enjoy reading this book together. This book was birthed as a way to share my family's story with others and for my daughter Sheriauna to have a voice. My hope is to create awareness in children from a young age about people with differences so that they can become more tolerant and accepting of others. Hopefully this is a great resource to open up a dialogue with your children about people with amputations and answer their questions in a safe environment.

Note to Teachers:

You have such a large role in the lives of our children as you teach them and interact with them during a large part of their day. Please use this book to create an opportunity to discuss differences, curiosity and questions vs. jeering and staring. You may not have a child in the class who has an amputation but your students will come across a child or adult one day who may have a mild or severe disability and my hope is that one conversation, one book, may make a difference.

Some words are highlighted in BLUE. Please see the glossary at the back of this book for definitions as a tool to help explain some of the technical words to readers.

My name is Sheriauna

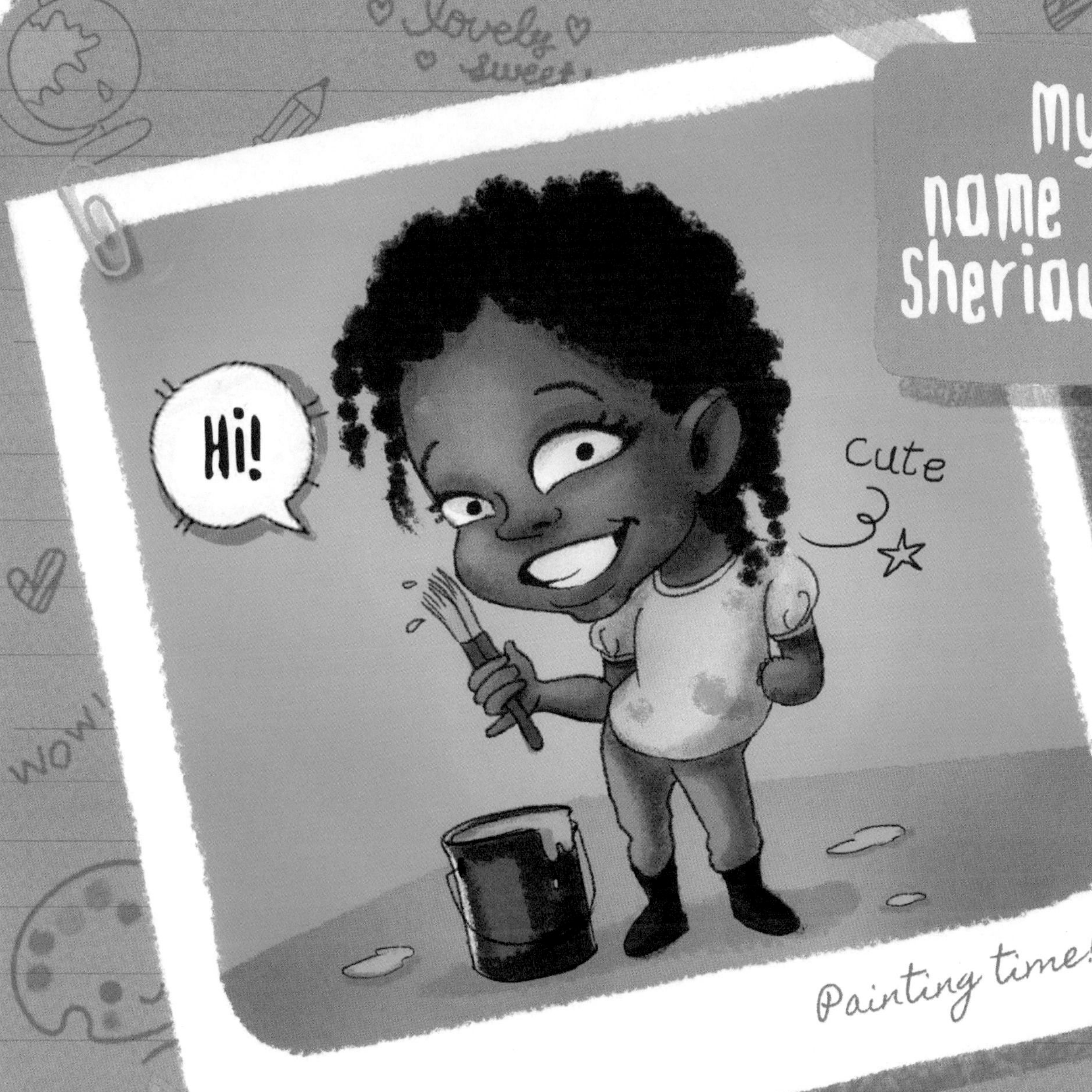

and I am four years old.

When
I was
in my
mommy's
tummy...

...the doctor said that
I was going to be born
without my left hand.

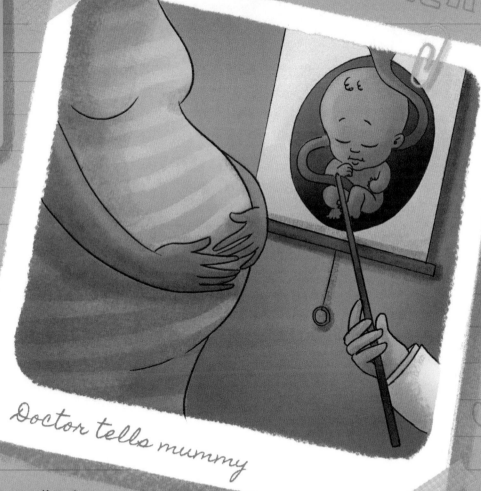

Doctor tells mummy

The doctor called it
a congenital limb reduction.

I loved to...

hold the telephone and say "Hi!" while holding my favourite teddy bear in my left arm.

I had different ways of doing some things but my difference never stopped me.

I was a handful **and more!**

Hello hello!!

when we go to the mall people stare at me.

I don't like it but Mommy says that sometimes people are curious because I don't look like them.

Sometimes grownups stare too and that makes Mommy sad because she just wants to protect me like all mommies do.

When I was 18 months old...

I went to a special hospital called Holland Bloorview, that helps children with differences and guess what?

They made me **a hand!**

It is called a prosthesis.

Say it with me, **pros-thee-sis.**

Basically it's an artificial device that replaces a missing one.

I have an artificial arm that I can use to help me do things everyday!

little ballerina!

But I just call it my helper arm because it's mine.

SCHOOL Rocks!

It helps me do cartwheels or ride my bike; I just have to keep practising. Now I use different attachments that can help me do different activities.

I still do things without my helper arm as well.

Kids do look at me...

...and are surprised when they see that I do not have a left hand.

but once they get to know me they just like me for me.. Not having a hand doesn't mean that I am any less able to be a kid.

I am beautiful...

...and wonderfully made!

It would be pretty boring if we were all the exact same right? We are all different and that's what makes us special. Until next time, please be kind to others :)

my Style

love you always!

I am Amazing!

GLOSSARY

Prosthesis: pros-the-sis (-sez):
1. An artificial device used to replace a missing body part, such as a limb, tooth, eye or heart valve.
2. Replacement of a missing body part with such a device.

Amputee: A person who has one or more limbs removed by amputation.

Congenital: Of or relating to a condition that is present at birth, as a result of either heredity or environmental influences.

Limb: One of the jointed appendages of an animal such as arm, leg, etc, used for locomotion or grasping.

Loss: The condition of being deprived or bereaved of something or someone.

Congenital Limb Loss: Deprived of a joint appendage (i.e. arm) at birth.

Nubbins: A small stub or stunted piece

Thanks and Gratitude.

To my Creator - When I saw the vision of Sheriauna I didn't know at the time what you were doing but I never thought for a moment there wasn't a reason. I prayed for direction to focus in on my purpose and I thank you for showing me through this process what I am meant to do. Sharing with others through the written word is beautiful and I look forward to sharing more with the world.

My wonderful family (Mom, Dad, Tonya and Mark) - You have all been a tower of strength and encouragement to me from the very beginning. Sheriauna and I are blessed to have you in our corner. The love and support we give each other is reciprocal and will continue. The African proverb says, "it takes a village to raise a child"; you are my village! xoxo

Jeffrey - As Sheriauna continues to flourish and inspire others with her kind heart, beautiful soul and her gifts, it reminds me that as much as we teach her she teaches us everyday. We are doing something right!

Rick and Shane - As timing would have it thank you for pointing me in the direction of two special people who are a part of this book.

My family and friends - For every personal call, message, comment or social media like, thank you. Your care and encouragement for Sheriauna is sincerely appreciated.

Ana and Mukul - After many obstacles and searches for just the right illustrator over several years, we connected and I could not have imagined doing this with anyone else. You were both so supportive and understanding during this process. I appreciate all the work you did to bring my vision to life. To see my daughter's face light up when I showed her the finished product was priceless and I thank you immensely.

Holland Bloorview and the Myo and Prosthetics staff - I am so grateful for your enthusiasm and embracing this book and the message right from the start. The work that you do to create ways that children can participate in life in many ways someone with all of their limbs takes for granted is so very important. The ability for a child to experience inclusion goes so much deeper that just the physical; their emotional, psychological and social well being are key. The way you interact with your clients and the atmosphere you create through a culture of inclusivity is what we need more of in this world.

The War Amps - for being there to assist families navigate through different stages of having a child amputee and for also providing financial support for those who need it, thank you.

10% of the purchase price for each book sold will be donated to Holland Bloorview Kids Rehabilitation Hospital and The War Amps. For more information about these organizations please visit their respective websites: hollandbloorview.ca | waramps.ca

Made in the USA
Middletown, DE
23 December 2020

30031257R00022